A GUIDE FOR
YOUNG SOFTBALL PITCHERS

ALSO BY DON OSTER

A Guide for Young Pitchers
with Bill McMillan

A Guide for Young
Batters & Baserunners
with Bill McMillan

All from The Lyons Press

A GUIDE FOR
YOUNG SOFTBALL PITCHERS

Don Oster and Jacque Hunter

THE LYONS PRESS
GUILFORD, CONNECTICUT
An imprint of The Globe Pequot Press

The Lyons Press is an imprint of The Globe Pequot Press.

10 9 8 7 6 5 4 3 2

Printed in the United States of America.

Library of Congress Cataloging-in-Publication Data

Oster, Don.
    A Guide for young softball pitchers / by Don Oster and Jacque Hunter.
    p. cm.
    ISBN 1-59228-734-4 (trade paper)
Pitching (Softball) I. Hunter, Jacque. II. Title.

GV881.4.P57O78 2004
796.357'8—dc22

2004065028

CONTENTS

ACKNOWLEDGMENTS

I want to take this opportunity to thank all of my former players and their supportive parents, without whose contributions and hard work this book would not be possible. I am also indebted to all of my present and former assistant coaches, especially Dennis Richardson and Don Sisloff, for their help in twenty-plus seasons.

I am grateful for Robert Holmes, former superintendent of the New Albany–Floyd County Consolidated School Corporation in Indiana, who had far-reaching vision in promoting athletics for young women.

And finally, thanks to New Albany High School Athletic Department and Don Unruh, athletic director, for the use of the facility where we took the photos for this book. Thanks also are due to Diane Carter, who endured my efforts on this book, and Kristi Clover, Jourdan Sparks, and Brittany Wiggington for their assistance in the photo process.

—*Jacque Hunter*

A GUIDE FOR
YOUNG SOFTBALL
PITCHERS

INTRODUCTION

Good softball pitchers aren't born; they are developed. You can become a good pitcher, a winning pitcher, and have a lot of fun along the way. It isn't necessary for you to be the biggest, strongest girl on the team to be a pitcher. A good pitcher can be any different shape or size. But good pitchers have a couple of things in common. First they really want to pitch. Second, they are willing to spend the considerable time and effort to condition, train, and develop their skills. To become a good pitcher takes a real strong commitment. First, ask yourself if you want to pitch badly enough to work hard to learn and develop. If you don't want to make the commitment, you might consider playing an outfield position.

Fast-pitch softball, at all levels, is basically pitcher-dominated. Very few really successful teams lack good pitching. There are several attributes that most good pitchers possess. They can control their pitches, throw strikes, and throw them with speed. They also have good self-control. Unruffled under pressure, they always give their best. And finally the best pitchers know how to win. As good team players, they have their head in the game and use their abilities to contribute to a successful team effort. And finally, good pitchers have fun doing their job.

This book is for those who are willing to pay the price in terms of hard work, dedication, and discipline to become a good pitcher. It will get you started on the right track to success. First, there is a chapter on getting in shape to pitch. To be effective, you must be in good physical shape. This chapter will outline exercises to help you get in shape and stay in shape during the season.

The next chapter covers pitching mechanics. It will show you how to make a smooth, consistent, effective delivery. You will learn how to use the pitcher's plate, your stride, and your arm to efficiently deliver a pitch. Chapter 5 covers how to throw different pitches. A softball can be thrown to curve much more than a baseball. A breaking pitch with a softball can be thrown to curve in any one of four directions. It is fun to watch batters whiff at a good drop or rise ball.

To become a good pitcher, you must be in shape and practice, practice, practice. Chapter 6 contains practice drills that will help you develop sound mechanics, an effective delivery, and good pitch control. Chapter 7, "Control," deals with two aspects: control of your pitches and self-control. You must be able to throw strikes (i.e., pitch control), and you also must be able to control your emotions in the heat of a game. Chapter 8, "Game Preparation," deals with preparing to pitch in a game. You want to be both physically and mentally prepared to do your best. This includes learning about the other team, pregame warm-up, and focusing on the task at hand.

Fooling batters is just about the most fun a pitcher can have. It isn't always done with a blazing fastball either. In Chapter 9, "Pitching to Batters," we cover sizing up the other team's batting order and how to pitch effectively to different types of hitters. Chapter 10, "Pitching to Win," describes the attributes of winning pitchers. Winning isn't all about pitch speed or breaking pitches; you also need to be a smart pitcher. The part between your ears is more important than any pitch. Having your head in the game will separate you as a pitcher from all the others who just throw pitches. As soon as you release a pitch, you become a fielder. If you are weak at fielding your position, teams can bunt you crazy. In chapter 11, we'll show you how to do your part on defense. Your commitment to practice what you'll learn in this book will start you on a path filled with fun and success as a good pitcher.

The last chapter provides some final thoughts about your development and where a pitching career might lead. We live in a wonderful age for female athletes where opportunities are abundant. As you start your pitching career, high levels can certainly be within your reach.

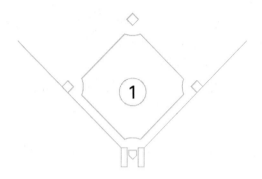

FAST-PITCH SOFTBALL

Fast-pitch softball is well named. Softball doesn't fit the name at all because the balls are definitely not soft; ask any umpire. Fast-pitch differentiates the game from slow-pitch softball where the pitch is lobbed over the plate. However, fast-pitch does relate to pitch speed, and that is what we will deal with here. There is no attempt here to turn young pitchers into speed freaks before they develop good sound mechanics and pitch control. But it is important to gain an understanding of the benefit of pitch speed in competition. Never forget that a pitcher's best pitch will always be a strike. This is true regardless of the pitch's speed or movement. However, unless you're throwing an off-speed pitch like a change-up on purpose, the faster strike is usually the most effective.

As a young pitcher you should concentrate first on developing the proper mechanics. A good, smooth, powerful delivery is the base of pitching technique that you will use throughout your pitching career. Also, you must learn to consistently throw strikes at whatever speed you can muster. No amount of speed will ever make up for poor control. It will be stated again in this book, but remember there is no defense for bases on balls. Early in your pitching career you will be pitching against players in or near your age group. Their hitting skills won't be very highly developed. If you can throw strikes at almost any speed, you will win most of your early games. However, as you get older and play at higher levels of competition, you will need to improve both the speed and control of your pitches.

You start your pitching career from a forty-foot distance. You will stay at this distance through high school. Unlike baseball pitchers, the distance or the rules don't change. A baseball pitcher throws from forty-six feet through age twelve, and runners can't lead off base. At thirteen, the baseball pitcher's world changes. The pitcher's plate on the mound moves to a little more than sixty feet from the plate, and runners can lead off.

You, however, start pitching at forty feet and stay at forty feet with no runners leading off base.

As you continue to practice, develop, and grow stronger, your pitch speed should increase. The batter's strength and skills will also improve. Here we will examine the advantage over batters that increased speed gives the softball pitcher. Batters need time to react to effectively hit your pitches. Simply put, the faster you pitch, the less reaction time they have. The forty-foot pitching distance is measured from the back tip of home plate to the front of the pitcher's plate. When a pitcher goes through her motion and delivery, the distance from release of the ball to the front of home plate is about thirty-eight feet.

If we apply simple math to different pitch speeds, a batter's reaction times are as follows: a thirty-mile-per-hour pitch allows a batter about nine-tenths of a second to react. At forty miles per hour the reaction time is approximately two-thirds of a second, or about one-fourth less time than the thirty-mph pitch. At fifty miles per hour, the reaction time is a little more than one-half of a second. In the allowed reaction time of a pitch, the batter must decide whether or not to swing. This includes a decision on pitch location, then activating the reflexes to swing and make contact with the ball.

More speed gives you an added advantage as long as you can throw strikes. But, high speed alone can be timed and hammered by good hitters. We want you to become a smart pitcher, not just a fast pitcher. Later in this book we will talk about spotting pitches and changing speeds to mess up a batter's timing. Consistently throw good, hard strikes, and you have the base to become a smart, winning pitcher.

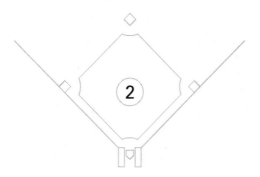

PROFILE OF A GOOD PITCHER

She knows she will be the starting pitcher. During the day she hasn't participated in any really strenuous activities. She has saved her energy for the game. When she arrives at the ballpark, she starts loosening up by jogging and doing some light stretching exercises. Then she teams up with her catcher to make her warm-up pitches. Starting slowly, she works up to full speed, concentrating on throwing strikes and hitting the catcher's target. Next she goes to the dugout and confers with her coach and catcher about the other team. They discuss the other team's strengths and weaknesses and how they will pitch to certain batters. This pitcher is physically and mentally prepared to pitch her best.

It's game time; Coach hands her the ball. She wants to pitch badly enough to fight the coach for the ball if necessary. She strides to the pitcher's plate and inspects the dirt around it. She grooms it to her liking then begins her warm-up pitches. Her face shows no sign of nervousness or emotion; she is very direct and businesslike. No observer would doubt that this is where she wants to be and she's really enjoying it. This is a very confident pitcher.

When she takes her warm-up pitches, they are crisp and in the strike zone. Her motion and delivery are smooth, simple, and powerful as she pushes off the pitcher's plate. Her arm is loose as she pitches. Her legs feel powerful. She feels like she could pitch all night if necessary. Throwing strikes is not a problem. In any control drills she can easily throw seven or more out of each ten pitches for strikes. Walks will be few. Batters will need to hit their way on base against her stuff. This is a well-conditioned pitcher throwing with excellent mechanics.

Even when she's at her best, the pitcher knows she won't strike out all of the batters. Those batters who hit the ball will be put out by her defense. The pitcher will know the game situation at all times and will call the number of outs and the plays, such as "one out, force at second" or "two outs, the play is at first." The pitcher encourages and trusts her defense; she is a good team player.

The pitcher knows that stuff happens in ball games. There will be some hits and an error once in a while. Runners will get on base, threatening to score. No matter how grim the situation may become, the pitcher will stay focused on her job. She will remain cool and not get rattled, but will bear down to get out of the jam. This pitcher has good self-control.

The pitcher and catcher always know where they are in the other team's lineup. They have scouted the other team and know the best hitters. They will work together to spot pitches that are hard for these batters to hit. The weaker hitters in the bottom of the batting order will be taken care of with a minimum of fuss. The pitcher isn't necessarily the fastest in the league, but she knows when to change speeds to keep the batters off balance. She has her head in the game; there is a reason for each pitch she delivers. This is a smart pitcher.

To summarize, this is a well-conditioned, smart pitcher with good, sound mechanics who focuses on her job. She has good pitch control and good self-control; this is a winning pitcher.

So this is what you will strive for. How do you get to this point? It will mainly be through practice, lots of it, hard work, and commitment to the task. It will also be by studying and learning to think the game. But it all starts with you. You must have the desire to become a good pitcher. The discipline and dedication necessary to excel can only come from one who wants it enough.

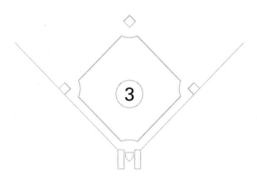

GETTING IN SHAPE TO PITCH

A young athlete shouldn't ever be in bad physical shape. Most will play more than one sport at an early age, keeping them busy throughout much of the year. Other activities such as swimming, riding a bike, or dance classes help keep muscle tone and flexibility. The following training routine for the legs is specifically for a young pitcher.

Any athlete must be in good physical condition to perform at his or her best. And this definitely applies to softball pitchers. There is a common misconception that a strong, quick arm is the ticket to success for a softball pitcher. However important the arm is, a pitcher will be effective only as long as her legs hold up. The legs and their strength are the base the pitcher operates from. They provide a thrust of power as the pitcher pushes off and delivers each pitch. High endurance in the legs allows a pitcher who is in good shape to last well beyond the regulation seven-inning games and/or pitch multiple games in a short time.

Conditioning is a must for pitchers of any age; it will separate average pitchers from really good ones. Everyone has ideas and suggestions about training and conditioning. At a minimum a pitcher should run every day except on a game day. But this would be during the season. To get in good preseason shape, we recommend that a serious training program begin at least three months before the season starts. Entering into and staying with a serious conditioning program will test your desire to become a good pitcher. None of this will be easy, but to be a good performer, it takes a strong commitment.

Remember to do some light calisthenics and stretching exercises before getting into each workout. Go easy at first; listen to your body. It will tell you if you're overtaxing it. An injury such as a pulled muscle can set you back for weeks. Overdoing can be harmful, so the following routines are meant as guidelines, not absolutes. Also, before entering into a rigorous training schedule, you may need to consult a physician. And you may need to lighten the time and repetitions if you are younger. Remember, the object is to get your legs and body in shape to pitch well. One program won't work for everyone.

Two training options are specifically for the legs. The simplest is riding a stationary bicycle, which can be done in any weather and is a good option for early season workouts. During the first month, ride the bike for up to sixty minutes three times each week. As soon as this is comfortable, increase to seventy-five to ninety minutes per session. Continue this routine through the following two months. Do each session nonstop with moderate resistance. Remember to drink plenty of water while riding. Walk for about fifteen minutes to cool down after each session.

The second option includes running a distance, running wind sprints, and doing aerobic exercises. During the first month run a half mile at moderate speed three times a week. Following a cooldown walk, run five twenty-yard wind sprints at full speed. Following another cooldown walk, do fifteen minutes of aerobic exercises. During the second month run three-quarters of a mile, run ten wind sprints, and continue the aerobics. Extend your distance to a mile in the third month. Run fifteen wind sprints and do the aerobics through the last month.

Either of the previous two programs, even if slightly modified, should certainly have your legs in good condition by the season's start. A third option for slightly older pitchers (junior high and high school) includes the bike riding or running activities, wind sprints, and aerobics in the first two programs, combined with training routines using light-weight dumbbells and barbells. The key is to use light weights. More repetitions with light weights will improve muscle tone and endurance.

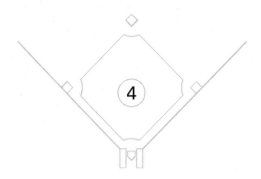

PITCHING MECHANICS

GETTING A LEGAL START

Before describing more detailed parts of pitching mechanics, it is important that any young pitcher learns the elements of a legal pitch. According to high school rules, there are several requirements in a legal pitch that will be described here. (This is included because so many young pitchers are observed using an illegal delivery.) Your desire to pitch naturally leads you toward becoming a high school pitcher. Getting started correctly and pitching and practicing within the guidelines mean you won't need to make changes in your delivery as you grow and progress.

Setting Up — Taking a Sign

In this description, if you are right-handed, the pivot foot is your right foot. For lefties, the pivot foot is the left foot. Do not step on the pitcher's plate without the ball in your possession. Prior to starting the pitch, your pivot foot must be in contact with the pitcher's plate. The other foot may be in contact with the pitcher's plate, but it is not required. Both feet must be within the length of the pitcher's plate. Your shoulders should be aligned toward first and third bases. With the ball in either hand, take the sign from your catcher.

Take sign (front view)

Take sign (side view)

Starting the Pitch

Next bring your hands together in front of your body. Your hands must be together for at least one full second. They may either be still or moving. The pitch starts when you separate your hands or make any motion that is part of a windup. You may take one step backward on your nonpivot foot, but this must be done before the hands come together.

Hands together (front view)

Hands together (side view)

Hands break to initiate delivery (front view)

Hands break to initiate delivery (side view)

The Delivery

The pitch is delivered as you make your windup while taking only one step with your nonpivot foot toward the batter. Your pivot foot must remain in contact with the pitcher's plate and the ground as you stride forward. As you release the pitch, you will push off the pitcher's plate with your pivot foot. Usually the toe of your pivot foot will drag the ground as you follow through after releasing the pitch.

Stride toward plate (side view)

Stride toward plate (front view)

Release the pitch (front view)

23

Release the pitch (side view)

The pitch must be underhand. Before releasing the ball only one full revolution of the arm is allowed. You may drop your hand to the side and slightly behind your hip before starting the windmill motion. As you release the pitch, your wrist may be no farther from your body than your elbow. After you release the ball your arm must follow through toward home plate past the vertical plane of your body.

Follow-through (front view)

Follow-through (side view)

Other

You have twenty seconds to deliver a pitch after receiving it in the pitcher's circle. You may not continue a revolution of the arm after the pitch is released. You may use a resin bag on your pitching hand, but you can have no other substance on your hand or fingers. You may not have tape on your hand or fingers. Between pitches you may lick your fingers, but you must wipe them before touching the ball.

The rule book definition of a legal pitch does a good job of describing basic, sound pitching mechanics. However, there is more to sound mechanics than the legal description. The following are some other elements.

THE PITCHER'S PLATE

The foot must be in contact with the pitcher's plate as you begin the stride and delivery. Always push off the front of the plate with a powerful move as you stride toward the batter. If necessary, scoop out a little of the dirt in front of the plate to give you a good solid base for your toes and foot. Using this solid base will help your pitch speed. As you make your stride and delivery, look at where your toe was in contact with the plate. If you are getting a good push off of the plate, you will see a distinct mark in the dirt where your toe drags away from the plate.

The push from the pitcher's plate helps provide power on the pitch.

When you're getting a good push off the plate,
you will leave a distinct toe drag in the dirt.

BALANCE — STEADY HEAD — SQUARE SHOULDERS

Good balance is a necessary element to maintaining good pitch control. Keep your head steady during the entire delivery and focus your eyes on the target. Without a steady head you will not have good balance. An off-balance pitcher may throw the ball anywhere. Keep your shoulders squared, facing the batter. Dropping a shoulder during the delivery will also affect your control. Keep your shoulders level through the release.

STRIDE

Your stride should be consistent. You will make a strong move toward the batter when you push off of the plate. This is not a lunge but a strong, powerful move. You want your lead foot to go directly toward home plate with a consistent stride length. It may be helpful during practice to draw a line in the dirt from where you push off the plate toward home plate. After you make a pitch check to see if your lead foot is landing on the line consistently. If you're far left or right of the line, your control will suffer. You will also have control problems if your stride length varies.

STAND UP

You will generally stand up straight with your chest thrust forward slightly toward the batter when throwing a fastball and most other pitches. You want your back to be straight but not stiff. On the drop pitch you lean slightly forward as explained in chapter 5.

SMOOTH AND CONSISTENT

The delivery should be smooth, powerful, and consistent. It will be hard to have good pitch control before you have your body under control. To get to this point takes practice, lots of practice. In later chapters we will talk about control drills where you can dial in your mechanics. Repetition of good mechanics is the best way to gain the muscle memory that will keep you consistent.

RHYTHM

Some pitchers go through certain movements to start their delivery. One way is after the hands come together, the pitcher raises them to chest height, then brings the hands down as they separate to begin the windmill motion. Others do the same upward pump with their hands, then whack their glove against their upper thigh as they start their pitching motion. There are many other motions that pitchers use. If these actions help the pitcher initiate and develop a rhythm on each pitch, they are okay but not necessary.

High pump to initiate pitch

IN-HOME PRACTICE

You can practice your delivery in front of a full-length mirror at home. Go through each step of your mechanics slowly, watching your movements. Gradually speed up your delivery to full, normal speed. Keep your head steady and stay balanced and smooth through the follow-through.

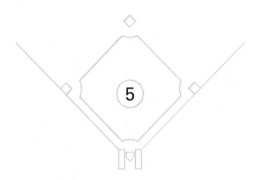

THE PITCHES

Make no mistake, your best pitch will always be a strike. However, in the following paragraphs we will describe and show you how to throw several different pitches. Most of these pitches will be somewhere between hard and impossible for very young pitchers to throw simply because of their small hand size. When your hand is small, just getting a firm grip on the ball will be about the best you can do. As you grow and your hand gets larger, you want to get the ball out in your fingers as far as possible while still maintaining a good grip on it. With the ball out on the fingers, using a wrist snap, you will be able to get rotation or spin on your pitches to throw breaking pitches as well as fastballs.

Grip the ball as far out in the fingers
as your hand size will allow.

THE FASTBALL

The fastball will always be your bread-and-butter pitch, no matter what level of competition you're pitching against. You learn it first in your pitching career and will probably use it more than all other pitches combined. You must be able to throw it for a strike most of the time and learn to spot it in different parts of the strike zone as you work batters. All of the other pitches you develop will play off of your fastball.

Basic fastball grip: across the seams

Basic fastball grip: with the seams

There are many ways to grip a fastball. First, the ball must feel comfortable in your hand. Second, your thumb and fingers, especially your middle finger, should have contact with the seams. You may throw the fastball with either a two- or four-seam rotation.

Fastball release

As you release the fastball, your palm is facing the batter. You snap your wrist and pull your hand upward. The ball releases off of the tips of your fingers imparting overspin toward the batter. Your follow-through will be with your arm extended and your hand palm up.

Wrist flip

Follow-through

THE CHANGE-UP

The second most important pitch to learn is the change-up. You will learn much more about how to use this pitch in later chapters. For now, just know that changing speed from pitch to pitch is the best way to mess with a batter's timing. Many pitchers succeed through high school using only a fastball and a change-up.

Your motion when you throw the change-up should look exactly like your fastball. The faster you throw the fastball, the better your change-up will work. The change-up pitch speed should be somewhere between half to three-quarters as fast as your fastball. The batter who has your fastball timed and is committed to hitting it should be completely fooled by a slow floater.

Change-up grip

The simplest way to throw the change-up is to bury the ball deep in the palm of your hand. You will find it difficult to get good speed from this grip, and it will also lessen the spin on the pitch. Although you want the change-up motion to look exactly like your fastball, the release is different. When you release the change-up, keep your hand and arm close to your hip. At the release point your hand should turn palm inward toward your hip. It is similar to reaching out to shake another person's hand. Sidespin may cause the pitch to break, but the speed difference is what makes a change-up most effective. Also always try to keep your change-up low in the strike zone. A batter who reacts to the speed change will find the low pitch harder to hit.

THE DROP BALL

A good drop pitch makes it hard for batters to make solid contact with the bat. It will usually result in infield ground balls at best. You want to also keep this pitch low. A good drop low on the outside corner of the plate or inside just off the kneecaps is a very difficult pitch to hit for even the best hitters.

You may throw the drop ball with either a two-seam or four-seam grip, whichever is most comfortable.

Drop grip

Drop release

Follow-through

When the drop pitch is released, roll the hand over the top of the ball as it passes your hip. You want to give the ball overspin. The release may feel like you're pushing the ball toward the ground. You should bend slightly forward at the waist at release. After the release your hand and arm will be slightly in front of your body as you follow through.

THE CURVEBALL

This pitch will break sideways through or around the strike zone. The release of a curve is later than it is for the drop pitch. It is thrown with the ball out on the fingertips. Keep your back straight as you make the pitch. To release the curve, you give it sidespin by turning your hand slightly toward your body as it passes your hip. Your arm pulls across your body through the motion. Your arm will be in front of your body as you follow through.

Curveball grip

You may throw the curve down the middle of the strike zone and break it outside. This makes a good sucker pitch for batters to chase. Another good location for the curve is thrown inside to break over the inside corner of the plate. As with almost all other pitches, the low curve will be hardest for the batters to hit.

Curve release

Follow-through

THE RISE BALL

This is the most difficult pitch to learn to throw. Grip it to get good seam contact with your thumb and fingers. You may even make seam contact with the nail of your index finger. To make the ball rise, you must release it so it will spin backward. In your windup you cup your wrist slightly and start to release the ball with the back of your hand pointed toward the batter. You flip your hand upward at release to give the ball backspin. Then you follow through with your arm extended high toward a twelve o'clock position.

Rise ball grip

Rise release

Follow-through

MIRROR DRILLS

It is helpful for a young pitcher to go through the delivery of pitches in slow motion. Going through deliveries in front of a full-length mirror is a good way to work on the mechanics and motion of the different pitches.

CLOSE-IN DRILLS

This is a drill to help you work on your mechanics, release point, and spin on pitches. Set up from six to ten feet from your catcher. Go through your delivery but don't throw hard in this drill. This is a good time to experiment with different grips. You may try anything to see how it works for you. The main points are comfort, ball in your fingers, seam contact, and a feeling of control with the grip you choose.

One of the first things to work on in this drill is your fastball release. This is a straight-off-the-fingertips release with a wrist snap and should be right at the catcher's glove. Once you feel confident with your fastball, work on the grip, hand position, and release of your change-up. Concentrate on these two pitches and get them right; they will be your mainstays throughout your career.

Close-in drill to work on releases and spin

Also work from this top release position in the close-in drill

SPIN

Next work on the breaking pitches. Working close without the pressure to throw strikes, you can concentrate on the release point and spin of the ball. Remember, the drop has overspin, the rise has backspin, and the curve spins sideways. If you have trouble picking up the spins in this drill, take a magic marker and put a couple of stripes on your practice ball. Once you start throwing breaking pitches, the spin drill should be part of a daily practice routine.

EXPERIMENT

One grip or technique won't work for all pitchers. When you are going through your drills, experiment with different grips, finger pressures, and releases. To be able to consistently control your pitches, your technique must feel comfortable. Work with your coaches, your catcher, and talk to other pitchers. Remember in working on breaking pitches that the spin and speed are the combination of elements that causes the ball to curve. Listen to suggestions; you may develop some pitches of your very own. In drills you may try anything; the test is if you can control a pitch and use it in game situations.

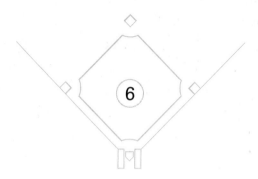

PITCHING PRACTICE

You started your conditioning program to get in shape at least at the first of the year. It is also the time to start pitching practice. (If you are already on a team, some of the parts of the following program may be done in team practice. However, this preseason training program is suggested for working out on your own.) You need a supply of balls, a place to practice, and a catcher. If you are one of the fortunate people who live in a warm winter climate, you can start outdoors. For those in colder spring climates, find an indoor place to practice. An area about fifty feet long with something to act as a backstop should work fine. You can cut out a home plate shape and fix a board on the floor or ground forty feet from home plate to serve as a pitcher's plate. You'll need a plate or solid object to push off from in your delivery.

The catcher could be anyone with the ability and time to work with you. It could be a friend or parent, but if the catcher is your regular teammate, it's a bonus. The more time you can spend developing and working together with your regular catcher, the more successfully you'll work as a team.

SET UP MARKERS

Make some markers to check your stride direction and length. Draw a line from where your back foot will be on the pitcher's plate during your delivery directly toward home plate. You will want your lead foot to land on or near this line. It will ensure that you're striding directly toward the batter. Make a pitch and mark the length of your normal stride toward home plate. Your lead foot should consistently land near this mark on each pitch. Lengthening your stride (lunging) or shortening your stride from pitch to pitch will affect your control. Check these markers anytime you start to have control problems.

WORK OUT ON A SCHEDULE

Try to schedule your workouts at least three times per week at the start. Begin each session with several minutes of warm-up exercises such as jogging, calisthenics, and stretching. You want to feel loose and warm before beginning your workout. Throw easy tosses to get your arm warm before starting to pitch. Pitch in sets of fifteen fastballs; then take a short breather. (Fifteen is the approximate number of pitches in an inning.) Start pitching at medium speed for the first week, working three sets each day. Have your catcher hold the target in the middle of the strike zone and count balls and strikes. Concentrate on keeping your good, smooth mechanics and do not try to aim the ball.

In the second week, throw two medium-speed sets; then throw harder in the third set. All of your pitches should be fastballs. Keep your mechanics under control as you throw harder. You should be able to throw ten or more strikes out of each fifteen pitches. Try to hold to this level of accuracy as you speed up your pitches. In the third week try throwing harder in all three sets while maintaining good accuracy. In the fourth week move up to five sets throwing hard in all of them. By now you should feel good in all workouts, and your conditioning will show. Listen to your body. If at any time you get twinges or soreness in your arm, stop immediately. Rest for a few days and start over with medium-speed pitches. Then gradually work back up to full speed as your body allows.

After working sets for a month, start spotting pitches. Have your catcher move the target into low inside and outside locations on the corners of the plate. Also have the catcher hold a high target about where a batter's hands would be. As soon as you can effectively spot pitches with a good ratio of strikes, start mixing in change-ups and breaking pitches. The objective through the second month is to get you ready to effectively work for six- or seven-inning sets, throwing a high percentage of strikes with all of your pitches. If you have followed an intensive conditioning schedule through this time period, you should be able to go this distance without tiring.

ADD A BATTER

Continue your workouts through the third month, refining control of your pitches. During your workouts, add a batter to the mix. Have a batter stand at the plate (wearing a helmet, of course), while you and your catcher work to different spots in the strike zone. Try to work to this batter as you would in a game. Keep a ball and strike count. The catcher should call for pitches and locations. Try to simulate game situations as much as possible.

If your control starts to falter, go back to the basics. Throw fastballs; check your markers and other parts of your mechanics. Perhaps your head isn't solid, you're bending your back too much, rushing your delivery, or dropping a shoulder. Your catcher or coach may be able to see some changes in your delivery and offer helpful suggestions.

OTHER DRILLS

During the third month, substitute a long-toss set for one of your regular sets once in a while.

Long toss

Move the pitcher's plate back and pitch from a longer distance. (Older pitchers may go back as far as eighty feet, or twice the regulation pitching distance.) Younger pitchers should start from fifty feet and throw a set, then move back to regulation distance and see if it seems to be easier to throw strikes. When you do the long-toss drill, move as far back as you can comfortably deliver the pitches. Working from the longer distances can also help strengthen your arm.

Some pitchers work out with a slightly heavier-weighted ball to help develop arm strength. They go through their normal delivery and pitch the weighted ball against a fence or backstop. And they may also use a lighter ball to help develop arm speed. This too is a drill where the ball is thrown into a fence.

FINALLY

So you're in good shape, can throw a strike anytime, spot your pitches, and change up when the situation warrants. After three months' work you should be anxious and ready for the season to begin.

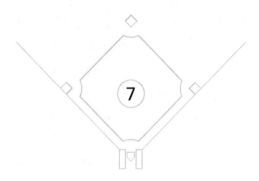

CONTROL

PITCH CONTROL

There are two elements to control for a young pitcher. The first is pitch control, which you have learned in drills and practice. Working with your catcher in fifteen-pitch sets, you should be able to throw strikes on about three out of four fastball pitches. This is good control, especially as you throw near your top speed. Once you attain something near this level of pitch control, it is time to move practice to another level. Mix in any of your breaking pitches and change-ups with fastballs and see if your control continues to be good.

In most cases there is no substitute for a strike. To be effective, you must throw a high percentage of strikes somewhere in the strike zone. But let's now explore a higher level of pitch control. This will take some help from your catcher. A pitcher throws; a catcher catches. If that's as far as the two of you go as a team, you're leaving a lot of potential success on the table. The two of you need to learn to act together as a team to work batters and get the most out of your efforts.

SPOT YOUR PITCHES

Most good softball pitchers throw hard. Fast enough, in fact, to blow the ball past many of the batters they face. There is another element to total pitching effectiveness, and it has to do with developing pinpoint pitch control. This drill simulates a game situation because you want your catcher to move the target (glove) into different parts of the strike zone. Think of the strike zone in four parts: low inside, low outside, high inside, and high outside are the four quadrants. Ask your catcher to hold the target in these areas as you practice. Strikes are good; low strikes are even better. Your ability to team up with your catcher to pitch into these zones will be an important part of working batters. This will be covered in chapter 9.

ADD A BATTER

Once you've improved at hitting different parts of the strike zone with only the catcher's target, add a batter to the drill. Now you have a real strike zone to work with. Pitch mostly to a low inside or low outside target. As you become accurate at hitting spots with a fastball, start mixing in breaking pitches if you have them and change-ups. Keep the change-ups low—even if the batter hits one, it usually is a harmless ground ball. Don't expect perfection in this drill, but the more you practice, the better you'll become.

WORK TO A LEFTY

You won't see a lot of left-handed batters. For some reason some pitchers with otherwise good control have difficulty pitching to a lefty. Have your batter stand in the left-handed batter's box and practice your pitches. The strike zone doesn't change, so get accustomed to working it the same as for a right-handed batter.

TRY WORKING LONG

When you're working on control drills, mix in the long-toss and short-toss drills. The regulation pitcher's plate is forty feet from home plate. Move back to pitch from a distance of about fifty feet. If you are throwing strikes from the longer distance, it will seem much easier when you move back to the regulation distance.

One final point: you're trying to nibble at the strike zone when you're pitching to spots. There is a tendency for pitchers to try to aim the pitch rather than going through their normal motion. *Do not aim your pitches.* Stay with your normal smooth delivery. You've worked hard to develop good mechanics; use what works for you.

SELF-CONTROL

The second major element of control is your own self-control. It is one thing to go through pitch control drills with a catcher with strike counts as the only challenge. But it is another matter altogether to keep your pitch control during the pressure of game situations. How well you are able to remain calm and focus on your job during games will have a great bearing on your pitching success. It is normal to be a little nervous or keyed up when you're pitching in a game. This shows that you really care about the game's outcome. As the key defensive player on the team, you know much of the team's success will depend on how well you perform. Pitching is your challenge. You must learn to channel all your energy toward throwing strikes and getting batters out.

Some days you will have your best stuff. You're hitting the corners, and batters are whiffing at your pitches and are totally baffled by your change-up. You're having fun, your team is winning, and Coach is happy. It's easy to focus, there isn't any stress, you're pitching at your best.

DEALING WITH STRESS

The real test of your self-control comes when it seems that nothing is going well. Some ball games seem to turn into mini disasters. Stuff happens like this: it's a close game with a team that's an archrival. You are pitching well, but your second baseman boots an easy ground ball. The next batter gets a squib hit to right field. The umpire blows a call on a full count to the next batter, which loads the bases. The other team's best hitter is coming to bat. Her teammates are screeching loud enough to move the dugout, fans are yelling all sorts of advice, and your coach is having fits. It is easy to blame someone else for the fix your team is in, but that won't help. It's your job to deal with it. If you can keep your cool in this situation, you have a main characteristic of a very good pitcher.

Many pitchers with high potential have failed because they can't deal with these high-pressure situations. Stress can affect pitchers in many different ways.

But usually pitch control will be no better than the pitcher's self-control when the heat is on. There may be a tendency to rush the delivery or try to aim pitches. Any of these stress-related changes in mechanics will only make a bad situation get worse. If you get rattled when the going gets tough, you will not be able to function at your best.

So how do you deal with this stress or tension that causes your muscles to tighten or makes your stomach churn? First step away from the pitcher's plate and take a couple of deep breaths. You should feel the tension lessening. Call your catcher out for a conference. Use the time to calm yourself. Remind yourself to focus on making good pitches and to trust your defense. You aren't alone: you've got eight teammates who will do their jobs. Above all, make the other team beat you with good hitting; don't get rattled and beat yourself.

Focus on getting each batter. You may get a comeback grounder and double play force-outs at home and first. With a strikeout you're out of the inning. Maybe in the next inning your teammates will go on a hitting spree and blow the game wide open. Think positive: this is a game, not the end of the world. They don't shoot the losing pitcher. The sun will come up tomorrow, and you'll do better the next time out. Like we said, stuff happens in ball games. Don't expect perfection because you'll certainly be disappointed. Learn to stay focused, stay cool, and take both good and bad breaks in stride. Remember what worked well and always try to learn from any mistakes.

RELIEF PITCHERS

Anything we've said about keeping pitch and self-control for a starting.pitcher goes double and more for a relief pitcher. The starter begins with a clean slate and may work into trouble. Starting clean at the beginning of an inning is the best a reliever can hope for. Unfortunately, a reliever likely won't be called on until a starter is in a fix and gets pulled. So, the relief pitcher goes into the game to deal with a mess that was developing while she was warming up or playing a position in the field.

Good relief pitchers look forward to taking on a challenge with runners on base and the game on the line. They have the mental toughness to go into a pressure situation and perform at their best level. Normally, the margin of error for a reliever is not big. Walking batters is definitely harmful. The reliever must throw strikes, challenge the batters, and trust the defense while maintaining her cool.

SUMMARY

Pitch Control

- ◆ Keep your smooth, powerful delivery
- ◆ Work with your catcher
- ◆ Spot pitches, work corners — mostly low
- ◆ Practice mixing pitches and speeds
- ◆ Don't aim pitches or rush your delivery
- ◆ Practice pitching to a lefty

Self-Control

- ◆ Focus on your job, be confident
- ◆ Relax, deal with tension or stress
- ◆ Stay positive
- ◆ Trust your defense
- ◆ Deal with one batter at a time

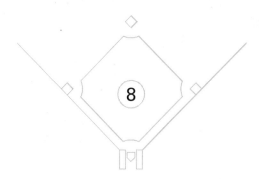

GAME PREPARATION

Game day is here; you know you're going to pitch. Part of your season will be during the school year. It isn't easy to put classes, friends, tests, and all the other potential distractions behind you and focus on a game, but you must try. Summer vacation offers another set of distractions that need to be dealt with to get mentally prepared for a game. It may be helpful to spend some quiet time by yourself to work into your game attitude.

On game day try to stay away from strenuous activities. Even if you're in great shape, you will need all of your strength to pitch your best. Stay out of a swimming pool. If it is a hot day, spend as much time as possible in a cool place. Again, on a hot day drink plenty of fluids;

dehydration can be a serious health problem. Eat early before the game. Allow your system about two hours to digest your meal.

STARTER

At the field try to start your warm-up routine about a half hour before game time. First, get your body loose by jogging and doing some stretching exercises using both your arms and legs. These exercises should be the same as you have done before workouts or practices. It is hard to say exactly how long you should take to warm up for the game. For most pitchers it takes longer to get good and loose when it is cool than on warm days. And some pitchers can be ready in a very short time, while others need a lot of pitches regardless of the temperature. You know your own timing best. Try, however, to time your warm-up pitching so you will have at least five minutes to relax before you go into the game.

Start the warm-up by throwing easy, increasing speed as you start to feel loose. Concentrate on keeping your good, smooth mechanics and throwing good pitches. Throw warm-up pitches only as long as it takes you to feel loose and throwing at top speed. Don't use yourself up during warm-ups; save it for the game. As soon as you can go at top speed with good control, go to the dugout and relax. It might also be a good idea to put a jacket sleeve on your arm to keep it warm. Once your muscles cool, they can tighten. You want your arm to be warm, loose, and ready when you enter the game.

RELIEF PITCHER

A relief pitcher may not be needed in a game, or she may be needed for any number of reasons. The starter could tire, get hurt, or become ineffective. The need for a reliever may come suddenly, allowing very little time for a sufficient warm-up. If the starting pitcher is injured, there is a provision that enough pitches are allowed for the replacement to warm up. However, a pitcher who enters the game for a reason other than an injury is only allowed eight warm-up pitches before facing a batter.

Find out from your coach if you are to be a relief pitcher in the game. If you're likely to relieve, warm up before the game enough to get loose. You must be mentally prepared to pitch on short notice. It may not be easy to stay focused. This is why good relievers are special. They can get in gear and be effective in a very short time. If you are a reliever and do not play another defensive position, the coach can send you out to warm up as a need arises. If the coach has the correct foresight, you should be loose and ready when you enter the game.

Position players who are also relievers have a more difficult time staying ready to pitch. For example, you're playing in the outfield. In the fifth inning the starter begins to lose her control. She starts going deep into the count on batters and actually walks a couple. A wild pitch and a hit batter load the bases with no outs. Your coach calls time-out, goes to talk to the pitcher, then calls you in to pitch. Coach gives you the ball. Now it's your ball game.

If you haven't taken the time to do some throwing between innings to stay loose, it may take a couple of batters for you to get up to speed. These are batters your team can ill afford to lose. Facing batters when you're cold in a game-breaking situation does not make for a good outing. Had you thrown a few pitches during the course of the game, you could be ready to throw strikes, focus, and give it your best.

THE PITCHER'S PLATE

The area around the pitcher's plate is your territory. Look it over before you take warm-up pitches. If it's not to your liking, fix it. If you aren't balanced when you deliver a pitch, your control will suffer. For example, you use the plate to push off in your delivery. The other team's pitcher may leave a hole in front of the plate that affects your balance. Make sure the plate is comfortable as a base when you make your warm-up pitches. If a hole needs filling, fill it yourself or ask your coach for help. Also examine the area where your lead foot will land. Make sure your foot won't slip as it lands. The same goes for the area around the pitcher's plate: get it fixed if it's not comfortable. Reexamine your territory each inning. It may need grooming each time you go out.

SCOUTING OTHER TEAMS

Good pitchers study batters. At a younger age you will likely be playing on a team in a league. One of the best ways to gain an edge is to scout other teams in your league. After you have watched a game or two, there should be few surprises when you face a team. By scouting you will learn the best hitters, the bunters, the slap hitters, the beggars, the lookers, and the weakest hitters. Watch for batter weaknesses to learn how to pitch to them. Note the fastest runners. These are the ones who may try to slap hit or bunt their way on base. More on this in the next chapter.

THE SCORE BOOK

A score book is kept by someone related to your team. Once you have played a team, there is no better place to study the batting order. Discuss the other team's batters with your catcher. Look at what the better hitters in the top of the lineup did, where they hit the ball—

anything that might help you spot a tendency. For example, a batter who always hits to the opposite field may want pitches on the outside of the plate. One who always pulls the ball may need an inside pitch. For these hitters tell your catcher where you want the target and how you plan to get these batters out. Look for the batters who habitually strike out and note if they are swinging or taking called third strikes. You may also find that the lower half of the team's batting order has given you very little trouble. You can dispose of them by simply throwing strikes.

Now you're warmed up, physically ready to pitch your game. You've scoped out the other team and know where you have an edge on their batters. Confidently put on your game face and go to the pitcher's plate. You're prepared to give it your best.

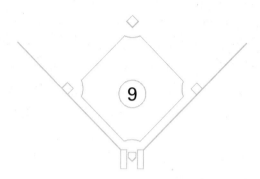

PITCHING TO BATTERS

You and your catcher are generally referred to as the "battery." The two of you provide the spark that starts and keeps things going in a game. How well you and your catcher work together as a team will have a great bearing on your team's defensive effectiveness. It would be good if you and your catcher read and study this chapter together. You and your catcher must "think" the game together. She is your strongest ally as she helps you size up batters and calls the pitches. Your catcher will see things about batters that you don't notice, things you can use to your advantage. Communicate with her during the game; she knows which of your pitches are working best.

All of your work getting into shape, developing sound mechanics, and working on speed and controlling your pitches comes down to pitching to batters. Fooling batters is what makes pitching so much fun. It's really what pitching is all about. Now is when all your control practice pays off. Your catcher calls pitches and sets her target where she wants them. Either through their stance or actions, certain batters will give clues where they have a batting weakness. The following are descriptions of different types of batters with suggestions on how to pitch to them. If your control isn't exactly great on a given day and you can't hit the spots, just throw strikes. Nothing is worse than trying to spot pitches, missing, and walking batters.

FIRST STRIKE

One of the best strategies when working batters is to throw a strike on the first pitch. This accomplishes two good things. First, you serve a little notice that walks are going to be hard to get today. Second, the strike puts you ahead in the count, which puts an added bit of pressure on the batter. There aren't many really good first-pitch hitters. And, many batters want to look at a pitch to try to time your speed before they get serious about hitting. Some batters may catch on to the good first pitch and come into the box ready to swing from the heels. If you see batters regularly going after the first pitch, bust a fastball low and outside or high and tight. The batter may chase anything out of the strike zone.

THE TENSE BATTER

You can see it when she steps into the batter's box. She looks nervous, tense, and you might even see white knuckles as she tightly grips the bat. As tension can work against you, here let it work for you. If this batter is tight when she steps in, give her some time to get even tighter. According to the rules, you have twenty seconds to deliver a pitch. (This rule is seldom enforced.) Use all of this time. Stand on the pitcher's plate and fake taking a signal or just stand looking toward your catcher. The time you take builds tension in the batter. Tension ties up the muscles, making it hard to take a good swing. With a little delay tactic, you can own this batter.

BEGGARS

Some batters show almost no intent to take a swing at the ball. They've been told to get on base and think they can draw a walk by just standing in the batter's box. They're actually challenging you to throw strikes. If a beggar does swing, it is usually a late, weak effort. Some will even crouch down in their stance to try to make their strike zone smaller. You will usually find these beggars near the bottom of the other team's batting order. Don't waste pitches on beggars. Give each one you face three strikes and a fast trip back to the dugout.

SLOW SWINGERS

You throw your first-pitch fastball, and the ball is in the catcher's glove before the bat gets into the strike zone. Or you again throw a good fastball, and the batter hits a weak foul to the opposite field. You've found a batter with a late swing, one that can't catch up to your fastball. Now, this is a good place for a rule of pitching that you must always remember: *Never throw an off-speed pitch to a weak hitter or a hitter with a late swing.* A change-up or other off-speed pitch is the only speed this batter is likely to be able to hit. Give this batter a load of good fastballs—she'll be lucky to foul one off.

PULL HITTER

The position of this batter's feet in the box will give the first clue to a pull hitter. The batter's stance will be open, the lead foot pointing down the third baseline for a right-handed batter, toward first for a lefty. This batter may start out with a straightaway stance, then stride down the baseline as the pitch comes in. The pull hitter wants an inside pitch to pull down the line. Many pull hitters have visions of hitting home runs, and once in a while one does when the pitch is inside where she can turn on it. Feed a pull hitter a dose of outside pitches. Very few batters have the strength to pull an outside pitch. Outside pitches hit by a batter trying to pull the ball usually result in weak ground balls to the infield.

THE ANXIOUS BATTER

Anxious batters look like they're hyped up. They dance around in the batter's box and take a lot of little half-swings like they're pumping themselves up. Some of these hyper batters are actually good hitters, their gyrations are meant to calm them to be ready to hit. Many of the anxious batters are ready to chase your first pitch. But if one is so ready, let her wait a bit. Give her some of the same treatment as the tense hitter, look a long time for a sign, then shake off a couple of signs from your catcher. Let the batter's tension build. Try throwing the first pitch out of the strike zone. She may chase any pitch. If she swings with or ahead of the pitch, she's a good candidate for a change-up. She may screw her feet into the ground when she misses it.

BIG, LOOPY SWINGERS

Watch batters take their practice swings. A loopy swinger will have her arms fully extended when she swings. Loopy swingers also tend to swing late. This is another batter you don't want to give a change-up. This batter wants a pitch down the middle or on the outside of the plate. Keep good speed on your pitches and keep them well inside the strike zone. Loopy swingers usually hit inside pitches on the bat handle resulting in harmless grounders and pop-ups.

CROWDING THE PLATE

This batter will set up where she is almost over the inside part of the plate. Her hands may even be in the strike zone. This batter may be looking for an outside pitch to hit, or she may be trying to take the plate away from you to draw a base on balls. This works on some pitchers who are so afraid of hitting a batter that they pitch away from a plate crowder.

You do not throw at batters. But, you have worked to refine your control. Remember the plate is yours. If a batter chooses to set up that close to the strike zone, inside pitches are going to be real close to her. Work her inside; low and inside is best. If you throw too far inside, she must get out of the way. A pitch that hits a batter in the strike zone is a strike. The most contact she makes on inside pitches will be weak handle hits. Shame on you if you let her take the plate away and you walk her.

SCARED BATTER

You usually find a timid, scared batter at the bottom of the lineup. The more pitch speed you have, the more scared batters you will see. Maybe the scared batter has been plunked a few times and wants no part of being close to your fastball. Scared batters sometimes have "happy feet." This means they may be set for the pitch but they bail out away from the plate as the pitch arrives. Sometimes this batter will set up with an open stance (front foot pointing down the baseline) or with a square stance but so far away from the plate that she can't possibly reach any outside pitch. Give her three strikes on the outside of the plate.

LEFT-HANDED BATTER/SLAP HITTER

You will face some natural left-handed batters. Their strike zone isn't any different; they're just set up on the other side of the plate. However, the first time you see a lefty at the plate be suspicious that she's a slap hitter. Slap hitters go from the left-handed batter's box. This position gets them two steps closer to first base than the right-handed batter's box. They take a short slap swing at the ball to hit an infield grounder and bet on their speed to beat the throw to first. A good slap hitter must have good timing and hand-eye coordination as well as good foot speed. You won't see very many really good ones.

The slap hitter will be starting to move toward first as she slaps at the ball. She will usually want a pitch down the middle of the plate or on the outside to drive toward third base. Pitches low and inside and high in the strike zone are hard for slap hitters to handle.

Don't let a slap hitter bother you; after all, she's trying to hit a ball your defense can handle.

THE GOOD HITTER

She steps confidently into the batter's box with a straightaway stance. She strides straight at you with the pitch. Her swing is level, tight, and compact. You'll find the best hitters on the other team at the top of their lineup. Good hitters may hit for power or hit to any field. However, unless you're facing a superstar, her batting average probably isn't as high as .400. This means you have, on average, a 60 percent chance of getting her out.

Pitch this good hitter carefully. Try to get ahead in the count. Mix speeds and move your pitches around in the strike zone. If it looks like she has your pitches timed, change speeds. You want her to hit your pitch. Many good hitters hate to draw a walk. They are aggressive, believing they can hit any pitch. If all of this fails, throw strikes, trust your defense, and make her hit her way on base.

BUNTERS

Players will bunt either to advance runners or to try to beat out a bunt for a base hit. You may expect a sacrifice bunt with runners on base and fewer than two outs. The bunter will square around and hold the bat out to contact the ball, sending it down a baseline. If the batter waits until your pitch is almost on its way, there is very little you can do other than field the ball and make the play. However, if the batter squares around early, throw her a high pitch. A high pitch is harder than a low pitch for the bunter to get down, and it may result in either a pop-up or foul tip.

FOUL BALL KEYS

Notice batters creeping toward the plate area when you're taking your warm-up pitches? They're trying to get a sense of timing on the speed of your pitches. Although batters are supposed to be in an on-deck area, umpires don't always make them stay there until they come to bat. While timing your pitches is important to batters, it is more important for you to know when they do have you timed. You can see late swings and those that are with the pitch. But foul balls can also give you clues when a batter has you timed.

A fastball foul that goes straight to the backstop is a signal that a batter is right on your pitch. The batter was with the pitch; she just didn't make solid contact. Try changing both speed and location on the next pitch. A batter that hits your fastball foul to the opposite field has a late bat. Don't throw this one a change-up; stay with the fastball and try to keep it inside. When a batter pulls your fastball foul, she is way ahead of your pitch. This may be an anxious batter or a pull hitter. Try change-ups to disrupt her timing and keep pitches on the outside part of the plate.

UMPIRES

You and the plate umpire each have a job to do. Each of you should go about your work with a minimum of interaction. Don't show any emotion or change of expression toward an umpire. Keep your cool and focus on your job. Umpires do not react favorably to pitchers who beg for strikes or protest calls. They also don't appreciate help from either pitchers or catchers. If an umpire makes a call that you think is bad, there is nothing you can do to change it. Just bear down and stick to your work.

Look for an umpire's bias in the strike zone. Some umpires will consistently call strikes on some pitches where you don't expect them. The location where the bias exists can be anywhere near the strike zone such as off an outside corner or a little low below the knees. When you and your catcher find a bias, use it. Work batters as you would normally, bearing in mind that a pitch in a bias location will usually be called a strike.

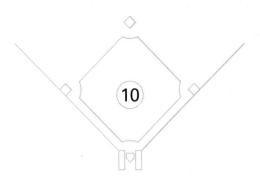

PITCHING TO WIN

YOUR CRITICAL DIFFERENCE

Throughout this book you have read chapters on conditioning, mechanics, pitches, control, game preparation, pitching to batters, and so on. There is one other element that is most critical to your success as a winning pitcher. Developing and learning to use that little six-inch area between your ears is what will separate you from other pitchers and make you a winner. A player with sound mechanics can go to the pitcher's plate and throw pitches. A pitcher also throws pitches but has a purpose or idea behind each pitch. The thought process, or having a reason for pitches, is what will separate you, the pitcher, from a thrower. The thrower just throws pitches. You must learn to pitch.

YOUR ADVANTAGE

When you go to the pitcher's plate, you have the advantage. There is an old baseball saying that good pitching beats good hitting. It is just as true in fast-pitch softball. The averages favor the pitcher and the explanation is simple. The best hitters you will face over the course of the season will not likely have a batting average above .400. This means that the best batters will get a hit only four times out of ten at bats. The other six times they do not get a hit. Most team batting averages including the best hitter are around .200. Simplified, this means two hits in ten at bats, which is about three innings. Additionally, this also computes to a team getting only five or six hits on average in your seven-inning game. And that's against all pitchers they've faced, few of whom are as effective as you.

The batter must hit a round ball with a round bat into fair territory where a fielder can't make a play. Her task is tough; you will make it much tougher when you're pitching. The final edge you have on batters is that you know what and where and at what speed your next pitch will be. The batter can only guess and react to what you throw. Depending on your pitch speed, the reaction time can be awful short.

You will win most of your games as long as you hold on to your advantage. Most of this is due to your performance. Another baseball truism that also applies to fast-pitch is "walks will haunt." You lose part of your advantage when you walk batters. There is no defense for a base on balls. Statistics indicate a high percentage of batters who get on base with less than two outs eventually score. This is why such importance is placed on throwing strikes. Another part of your advantage can be lost through fielding errors. This is a part you can't control. Your teammates will make some errors, and errors can lead to some lost ball games. To expect them to be perfect is not realistic. You must take fielding errors in stride. Respond by bearing down and getting the next batters out.

THE OTHER TEAM'S BATTING ORDER

You and your catcher must always know what part of the other team's batting order you are facing. You might ask your scorer what these batters did the last time you faced them. Their history against you should give you some clues as to how to pitch to them. You may be facing a team for the first time. If so, fall back on the makeup of a normal team's batting order, described as follows:

The leadoff batter's job is to try anything to get on base. She will usually be a fast runner and may have a small strike zone, hoping to draw a walk. This batter and the number two hitter may also try slapping the ball. The two through five batters will usually be the better hitters with the team's best of all in the three and four positions. Pitch to these batters carefully; they are the most likely to cause you trouble. Throw a first-pitch strike and keep the pressure on them by not going deep into the count. Mix up your pitches and pitch locations. Throw them your best pitches and change speeds once in a while to keep them off balance.

The lower batters in the lineup will be the weaker hitters on the team. Don't get cute with this part of the lineup. Do not waste pitches to these batters. Throw strikes and challenge them to hit their way on base. Do not walk one of these weaker batters; it can lead to trouble. You don't want runners on base when the top of the order comes to bat. Do not relax or let up because you're in the light end of the batting order. It's likely that you'll face this low end of the order three times in a seven-inning game. If you take them out each time, that's three of the seven innings you need for a complete game.

IT'S YOUR BALL GAME

When the coach gives you the ball, it's your ball game. Nothing happens until you make a pitch. You have control of the game, act like it. Let your confidence show in the way you handle yourself. Let them know you aren't going to be easy to deal with. Be businesslike as you groom your area and take your warm-up pitches. Act like you belong there and are really enjoying it.

Wear your game face. If you show any signs of nervousness, batters may think they've got you on the run and dig in deeper to hit anything you throw. Don't show any emotion; just concentrate on getting them out. You control the pace of the game. Use this as necessary to keep your self-control. You can also use a pause on certain anxious or nervous batters. You and your catcher select your pitches. The batters are at a disadvantage when they face you.

SPOT PITCHES

Most of the time you can throw strikes when needed. And this is what you do when you're pitching to the bottom of the batting order. The top half of the order will take a little more care. In the following two sections we talk about strategies for pitching to the better hitters in the top of the order. You have practiced pitching to spots. This is where all your hard work will pay off.

Spotting pitches works best when your control is on and you're not getting behind in the count. Most batters have a power zone at or above the waist. Have your catcher hold a low target for most pitches. There are very few good low-ball hitters. A low inside pitch at the knees is a difficult pitch to hit. If your drop pitch is working, a drop low on the outside corner is also tough to hit well. Have your catcher mix pitches low in and out. Once in a while burn a fastball right at the batter's fists. This usually results in a weak handle hit.

When you're working well low and are ahead in the count, try burning in a real high pitch. Many, even good hitters, can't resist going after a high pitch that's up around their shoulders. The real high pitch is a good strikeout pitch. If you can throw a rise ball, this is a good place to use it. When you're going high, be careful not to make it too good. A slip that locates the pitch around the batter's belt may get whacked.

MIX SPEEDS

Most teams take batting practice on a machine. Few coaches will set a machine to pitch low or nibble at the corners of the plate. The machine will be set to throw constant speed pitches down the middle of the strike zone. After a few pitches, the better hitters can time the machine and rip pitch after pitch. Not even the fastest pitchers can throw the ball past all the batters. These batters may train on some awfully fast machine pitches. If you always throw at a constant speed, the better hitters will time you just like they do the machine.

Winning pitchers mess with batters' timing. Mixing speeds and spotting pitches are your two best weapons to get good hitters out. Pitch smart by mixing speeds to keep batters off balance. For example, the other team's number four batter is at the plate. She pulls a fastball foul down the left field line. She's nearly got your fastball timed but is a bit ahead of it. This is a good time for your change-up. Your change-up can be either a straight or breaking pitch. You want it to be low and about 60 to 70 percent as fast as your fastball. Keep your windup and delivery looking like you're throwing a fastball and watch her swing before the ball gets near the plate. Use of a change-up confuses hitters. The threat that you'll use it is always there, and only you and your catcher know when it's coming.

To repeat the warning, don't change up on a bad hitter or late swinger. They only get your best fastball. Practice speed changes on breaking pitches as well as throwing your change-up. Reserve them for use on good hitters who are anxious and those who have your fastball timed.

WORK THE COUNT

Again, the first-pitch strike is very important. You want to get ahead in the count. A second strike really puts pressure on the batter. No batter wants to strike out. All of them come to the plate to hit except the lookers who are begging for a walk. Conventional wisdom is to throw a waste pitch out of the strike zone on an 0 and 2 count. The notion is that the batter will chase a bad pitch and strike out. This is pretty good advice when you're pitching to a better hitter. But don't waste pitches to a late swinger or bad hitter. Go with your good fastball.

You're still ahead when the count is 1 and 2. Pitch with care to a better hitter; try to get a corner call on a low pitch. If the count goes to 2 and 2, you want this to be a deciding pitch. Make the batter hit your pitch. If you miss and the count goes full, you lose some of your advantage. On 0 and 3, 1 and 2, 1 and 3, and full counts, throw strikes and trust your defense to make the plays. Remember, there is no defense for a base on balls.

LEARNING TO WIN

Winning pitchers use their head and think the game. They are pitchers not throwers. A winner knows her strengths and learns from her mistakes, then works to correct them. She knows where she has the edge and uses it to her advantage. It is a good habit to take the time to think about a game soon after it's over. Remember the things that went well and those that didn't. If you had problems, think of ways to correct them. Early in your career you may learn more from a loss than a win. Winning pitchers never stop trying to learn. You are just starting your pitching career, and who knows where it might lead? Using that little six-inch area between your ears is the key to making you a winner.

SUMMARY: THINGS TO REMEMBER

- Be confident, you have the advantage
- Be a pitcher not a thrower
- Know the other team's lineup
- Have an idea for your pitches
- Team with your catcher
- Spot pitches, mix speeds
- Never stop learning

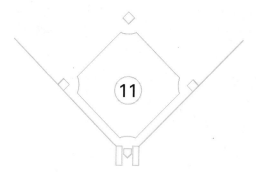

FIELDING YOUR POSITION

As soon as you release a pitch, you become a fielder. If your most important job is throwing strikes and dealing with batters, fielding your position well is definitely the next most important. Always be in a ready position to field a ball as you release each pitch and follow through. That is the instant when you become an infielder. Any batted ball hit to you is an opportunity to get an out. You only need to get twenty-one outs in a seven-inning game, and each one you help get as a fielder is one less batter you'll have to face later.

COMEBACK HITS

For some reason good pitchers get a lot of balls hit back to them. Some of these comebackers are hit hard, requiring you to be in a solid fielding position, ready to move quickly to field the ball. With no runners on base, the comebacker you field should be an easy out at first base. Practice fielding and making the throw to your first baseman until you both have confidence that it will almost be an automatic play.

Before you make each pitch when there are runners on base, you should know where to make a play if a ball is hit back to you. Remember, you always have a play at first. If there are two outs, the play is at first and you're out of the inning. But when there are fewer than two outs with runners on base, there may be time to cut down lead runners.

Because runners can't leave a base until you've released the pitch, you should have plenty of time to force lead runners when you get a hard comeback. With fewer than two outs and a runner on first, force the runner at second. With runners on first and second and fewer than two outs, force the lead runner at third. Again, with fewer than two outs and the bases loaded, make the force at home. Always make sure you get the lead runner. At times an infielder or the catcher may be able to make a throw to complete a double play. Cutting down lead runners can quickly kill the other team's offensive rally. Being able to make these plays takes practice and execution by all infielders and the catcher.

With runners on second or third but not at first, you don't have a force play other than at first base. When there are fewer than two outs and you get a hard comebacker, turn to look the runner(s) back. Pick off any runner attempting to advance. If they hold at their bases, throw to first to take the sure out.

Line drives and short, looping fly balls hit to you present an immediate double play opportunity when there are runners on base. Again, you must know the situation before making each pitch. Catch the ball and double off any runner who has moved off base.

SLOW ROLLERS

Wimpy, softly hit slow-rolling ground balls can be a challenge for a pitcher to handle. It is up to the pitcher's judgment, but there seldom is time to get a force play on a lead runner. You can never go too far wrong when you get an out, so go ahead and make a good throw to get the runner going to first.

POP-UPS

High infield pop-ups can trigger a real circus if the infielders don't communicate. A short, low, looping pop-up should be taken by the nearest infielder. In general, the pitcher will only handle pop-ups between her position and the plate, those that she moves forward to catch. The general rule is that a fielder moving forward to field a pop-up or fly ball will have the best chance of making the play correctly. Some coaches prefer that the pitcher not take pop-ups at all, requiring an infielder to call for ("I've got it!") and take all high pop-ups near the pitcher.

BUNTS

Almost any pitch can be bunted, and many teams use bunts as an important part of their offensive strategy. Bunts are used for two reasons: to advance runners or any attempt to get a base hit. Bunting is strategically good because it puts pressure on a defense to make a play. It is amazing how many times otherwise good fielding teams botch up a play on a simple bunt. Pitchers must absolutely be able to field and make plays on bunts. Any pitcher who is bothered by bunts or can't field them and make the plays can be quickly bunted off the field by a smart team.

Learning to field bunts effectively takes a lot of practice. You must be able to get to the ball and field it quickly, then make a quick, accurate throw to the base. With most bunts, the only play is to first base because there isn't time to force a lead runner. However, you may have a force play with runner(s) on base if the ball is bunted hard right at you.

Bunt defenses vary and are usually set up by the coach. However, the catcher usually takes all bunts that travel no farther than two steps in front of home plate. There may be a special setup for sacrifice situations in which the first and third basemen play in to take bunts down the lines and you handle the rest. An attempted bunt for a base hit will likely be all yours to play because the first and third basemen usually won't be playing in on the lines.

Communication between infielders and the pitcher on bunt plays is critical. The player who is going to field the bunt must call off the other fielders ("I've got it!"), similar to calling for fly balls.

COVERING BASES

It is the pitcher's responsibility to back up plays from the field on runners advancing toward third or home. Your position in either case should be far enough back of the base so you can field the ball and make a play on a runner if necessary. Try to anticipate if the play on a runner will be at third or home. If it is not clear, go to a point in foul territory halfway between third and home and move to back up the correct base as the play develops.

When there is a runner on third, you must cover home plate if a pitch gets past the catcher. To properly cover the plate, sprint to a point in fair territory about two feet up the third baseline from the plate. Stay in fair territory and set yourself to take the throw to tag the runner out as she slides toward the plate. Do not attempt to block the plate; collisions are potentially harmful to your body. Catch the ball and make a good, low tag by holding your glove in front of the plate.

FINALLY

It is helpful if at some time you played another position in the field. If so, you should have less trouble being able to field your pitcher's position well. However, skills alone are not enough. You must keep your head in the game, know the situations and where to make the right plays. The other ingredient to success is that you must hustle when doing your jobs. Remember, you can either help or hurt your cause with your fielding.

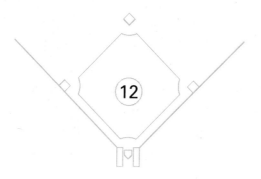

FINAL THOUGHTS

As the pitcher, you play the key position on the team. Fast-pitch softball at all levels, from beginner recreation leagues, even through college, is basically pitcher-dominated. Without good, effective pitching a team will have very little success. You have learned keys to pitching success in this book and can be well on your way to a career filled with fun. But, you will also need to learn to manage your expectations. Don't expect to strike out each batter you face—it won't happen. You must rely on your eight teammates to do their jobs and help you get outs. Don't expect to win every game—this won't happen either. Softball is a game of inches, and breaks go both ways. Give each pitch in each game your best and learn to accept the outcome with class. No one can expect any more than this from you. Learn from your mistakes, stay focused, keep your cool, and always remember to have fun.

In the introduction it was stated that this is a wonderful time for female athletes. Since the beginning of gender equity rules in athletics, opportunities that didn't exist a decade ago for female athletes have opened up. To apply this specifically to a young softball pitcher: one who develops into a highly effective high school pitcher will certainly draw notice. College coaches and scouts scour high schools looking for pitchers with good potential. The possibility that an outstanding high school pitcher may receive a college scholarship offer is very real in today's environment.

ABOUT THE AUTHORS

Don Oster is a longtime baseball coach and current Indiana high school baseball and softball umpire. His Babe Ruth League team, for which he was the pitching coach, appeared in four consecutive World Series. He is also the author of *Largemouth Bass,* and coauthor of *A Guide for Young Pitchers; A Guide for Young Batters & Baserunners;* and *Hunting Today's Whitetail.* He lives in southern Indiana.

Jacque Hunter, a veteran of twenty-eight years at New Albany High School in Indiana, was inducted into the Indiana High School Coaches Hall of Fame in 2003. During his coaching career, his teams have made six appearances at the state finals, have been state runner-up twice, and won one Indiana State Championship. In 1996 he was the first coach in Indiana to record 300 victories, and his teams notched number 400 in 2003. After the 2004 season, his overall coaching record stood at 425 wins and 138 losses. Coach Hunter is a two-time State All-Star Team Coach and has received numerous Coach of the Year honors at the district, conference, and state levels.